VINCENT ELDON

RULES FOR LIFE

**The Ultimate Guide On How to Live a Balanced
Life, Discover the Best Ways to Balance Various
Areas of Your Life to Get the Most Out of It**

Descrierea CIP a Bibliotecii Naționale a României
VINCENT ELDON
    RULES FOR LIFE. The Ultimate Guide On How to Live a Balanced Life, Discover the Best Ways to Balance Various Areas of Your Life to Get the Most Out of It / Vincent Eldon – Bucharest: Editura My Ebook, 2021
    ISBN

VINCENT ELDON

RULES FOR LIFE

The Ultimate Guide On How to Live a Balanced Life, Discover the Best Ways to Balance Various Areas of Your Life to Get the Most Out of It

My Ebook Publishing House
Bucharest, 2021

TABLE OF CONTENTS

CHAPTER 1

WHAT IS A BALANCED LIFE?

How many times have you heard people say that they would love to balance out their lives? Probably quite a few and no doubt you have said the same thing to. But what is a balanced life anyway? Let's take a look.

When your life is balanced you feel happy about those things you do and about who you are. You don't feel overwhelmed when unexpected things crop up.

In order to live a balanced life then try to use the following five habits and apply them to your own life.

1. While it is important to plan for the future you do need to be aware of what is happening in your life right now. So awareness is the first habit you need to form. When your life is balanced it means that you are aware of your current situation, it does not mean being obsessed with what the future might hold.

It also means letting go of the past. Being aware allows you to make good decisions and choices, giving you fewer regrets later on.

2. The next habit is taking care of your body and your health. You need to be grateful for what you have and you need to take care of yourself to maintain this. This includes paying attention to what you eat and getting in enough exercise. This habit also includes learning to rest and relax when you are tired. If your body is not balanced then neither will your life be balanced.

3. Onto the next habit which involves your creativity. Every person faces some type of challenge almost every day. When you can learn to deal with these challenges by incorporating your creativity into them, you are well on the way to having a balanced life.

4. Your next habit is the one of patience and this can be difficult for many people to develop. By developing patience as a habit it will help you deal with almost all challenges, problems and issues that life loves to throw at you. Developing patience improves your own life and that of your spouse's and your children's lives. So learn how to not react immediately and quite often a simple smile can diffuse any situation.

5. Our lives are totally complicated and by simplifying them you can easily balance things out more. Try to think of what you must have in your life and do away with unnecessary things. Do you need to own two fancy cars, or go on that fancy vacation just because your friends do? Pick and choose what is important to you and your family in order to live a happy and fulfilled life.

CHAPTER 2

BALANCING THE VARIOUS AREAS
OF YOUR LIFE

For anyone who wants to create a balance in their life at home and at work there are various areas that you need to look at. You may not actually be aware of how all these different areas affect you when it comes to leading a balanced life.

The various areas of your life to look at include:

1. Spouse/Partner
2. Children
3. Parents
4. Relatives
5. Friends
6. Work
7. Colleagues

8. Boss

9. Your own health

Take a look at each area and determine if you are happy with each one. Things to ask yourself include questions such as:

1. Do I spend enough time with these people?

2. Do I get along with them?

3. Do I enjoy what I am doing?

4. Do I eat a healthy diet?

5. Do I exercise enough?

If there is an area that gives you an answer that you are not happy about, then this is a point that needs improvement. If you aren't exercising enough look for ways to improve this. Can you incorporate exercise into a family activity such as going hiking or swimming? This fulfills you in two areas, spending time on exercise and spending time with your family.

If your answer to the work question is no, that you dislike your job. Look for ways to correct this. Can you ask for a transfer to another department or even relocate to a new office? Or is it time to look for a new job altogether?

When you have even one area that you are dissatisfied with this can ruin any balance in your life. The above list of areas are only suggestions and you may have others that you want to include.

Simply create your own list of the people and things that are important to you. Then examine each one to see if you are happy with the current outcomes of each.

If not, determine if a) how important they actually are and b) what you can do to improve this. Your actions could be to cross them off your list because after some debate they aren't as necessary as you thought.

When you have a balance in your life at home and at work you should always be:

1. Happy with your current situation
2. Able to deal with any curve ball life throws your way
3. Have a peace of mind
4. Be happy with the person that you are

So now it is your turn to start creating balance in your life, good luck.

CHAPTER 3

HOW TO BALANCE YOUR LIFE
AND YOUR JOB

It can be difficult to not bring/ home your work with you. You may have a demanding job or you may hate your job and you bring this home with you. Just how can you balance your personal life and your job without letting the other suffer?

While it is easy to say the minute you swipe out or get into your car to drive home, stop thinking about work. This is not always so easy to accomplish. If your job is demanding you may be tempted to bring work home with you. On the other hand if you dislike your job you feel like going home and ranting about it. Neither one is a good option.

When you bring work home it can interfere with the time you have to spend with your family. You may only intend to spend 30 minutes proof reading but instead this turns into a couple of hours. By the time you are done your kids are in bed and you wonder why they don't interact with you as much as they used to.

If you do nothing but scream and yell when you get home, this also has a negative effect on those around you. As much as they want you home they can start to dread that time.

To balance this out you need to take a good look at both situations. If your work load is too much is there a way to reduce it? Can you delegate some of your tasks to a junior member? Does your boss know that you are bringing home work?

Don't try and be a super hero and get everything done alone. It just isn't possible and your personal life as well as your health could suffer. Learn to prioritize what has to be done before you leave work each evening. This way in the morning you can look after the most important items first.

If you hate your job and do nothing but shout at your spouse or partner then maybe it is time to start looking for a new one.

Research has shown that going to a job you detest each day can put you into a severe depression.

Even driving to work can become dangerous. You are dreading arriving at work and may not be paying enough attention on the road. One day you just may not arrive at work or at home either. Is your job worth it?

TOP TIPS FOR BALANCING LIFE AND WORK

Just about everyone these days has to figure out a way to balance life and work. Use the following tips to help you achieve just this.

1. **Defining and Setting Your Priorities** - regardless of how much you would like to get accomplished each day, you only have 24 hours. For this reason you must learn to set your priorities. Take a look at all the things you want to get done including:

- Being successful at work
- Exercising more often
- Spending more time with your children
- Taking an evening class

Now you must determine which items are most important to you. If you want to spend more time with your children, then schedule certain time periods for this.

While you may want to take an evening class, how important is this to you? Are you trying to improve your education to get a better paying job? Or is it for pleasure - define and set your priorities.

2. **Planning in Advance** - there is no doubt that from Monday to Friday you are extremely busy. If preparing meals is difficult and you tend to resort to fast food, start planning and preparing meals on the weekend. You could cook up a large roast or chicken on Sunday. Use the leftovers for Monday's meal. Make up a large batch of soup or spaghetti and freeze some for during the week. With a little advance planning and preparing you can feed healthy meals to your family and reduce your eating out budget.

3. **Share Responsibilities** - this applies to both your job and your home life. If you are feeling overwhelmed at work is it possible to delegate certain projects to a co-worker? Talk to your boss about this, they may not even realize how overwhelmed you are feeling.

At home you don't have to be the super parent, there is nothing wrong with asking for help. Delegate chores to your children, even young children can help tidying up and vacuum.

If you and your spouse need a break ask another family member if they could watch your kids for the evening or weekend. When was the last time they stayed over at their grandparents? This can be a great way to free up some time to spent together and both your kids and the grandparents will love spending time together.

Use these top tips to add a sense of stability and balance back into your life. There is no need to feel overwhelmed at home or at work. Asking for help can bring you rewards you never dreamed of.

CHAPTER 4

BALANCING LIFE WITH YOUR CHILDREN

No one is going to deny that your children are not important to you. But one thing that you may be guilty of is devoting so much time to them that you have nothing left for you.

Wanting to be there for your kids is a normal parenting instinct. It is very easy to overdo this by giving them everything they want. This is very true if you work full time outside the home.

Many parents like to put their kids into after school programs, some do it to make up for not always being there for them. While your intentions are wonderful, have you ever considered if this is really what your children want? Have you taken the time to ask them if they would prefer to do an after school sport instead of spending more time with you? Their answer may just surprise you.

Try to limit the amount of after school activities that your children do. By enrolling them in lots of classes it just makes more work for both you and them. Your child may have trouble getting all of their home work done or just be too tired once they get home.

If you happen to be one of their coaches this commitment can really eat into your time. As well as your children's activities look at your own. Do you help out at Church or volunteer for a program or charity? While this is all wonderful it is not always the best idea if you are trying to balance your life with your children's.

Many parents do struggle trying to create a balance with work and their children. One way around this is to actually discuss your work with your children. This way they can understand why your time is limited and they can get a glimpse into what you do for a living.

When you can share what is going on at work with your children they will often offer to help out more at home. After all if they don't know why you are always home late or have to work after dinner they can't help you.

One important thing for you and your children to learn is to how to say no to certain things. If you are asked to help out at a function and really don't have the time, learn to say no. Don't feel guilty about this, feel positive that you are placing your family before others.

CHAPTER 5

LIFE BALANCING FOR TEENS

There is so much focus on balancing work and life for adults but not as much for teenagers. While teens may not be working full time jobs they still have a ton of pressure to deal with. They are trying to juggle school plus any after school activities, sports, part time jobs, any responsibilities that they have at home, then they are just trying to fit in socially with their friends.

It is important for teenagers to know that they have someone to talk to if they are feeling stressed out. As a parent, if you are feeling stressed out, talk about your feelings to your teenagers. This could be a great way to get them to open up to you. Let them know that they can approach you or a teacher at school if necessary.

Teens should learn how to set their own prioritises and to realize that they don't have to be a super student or over achiever. While most teens do have goals these need to be realistic goals.

To help your teen set priorities discuss with them what school assignments are due and when. Using an online calendar or app is a fun way to help them get organized. Show them your own priorities so they can see how you handle them.

If they have a lot of assignments to get through, instead of working on all of them each night, they may be better to tackle just one or two at a time.

All teens and adults, for that matter, what to be good at everything. They want to excel in their studies, they want to be good in sports or get the lead in the school play. This often leads them to being involved in way too many activities at one time.

Talk to your teen about selecting just one or two things that they really enjoy doing. Then focusing on just those, they will probably enjoy doing them more and will naturally excel at them.

The teenage years can be an extremely emotional time. As well as school work and pressure, their hormones can be playing havoc with their feelings. If you see that your teen seems overly emotional encourage them to discuss their feelings with someone. It is much better for them to speak with someone than keep their feelings bottled up inside.

Try to lead by example so that your teenager will have fewer issues when it comes to dealing with all the complexities that high school and just being a teenager holds.

CHAPTER 6

USING SPORTS TO BALANCE YOUR LIFE

Have you considered using exercise and sports as a way to balance your life? If not, it is something you should seriously think about.

Taking part in some type of sport can help you in many ways. First it allows you to take a break from your hectic day. Exercise is good for your mind as well as your body, it refreshes and reenergizes you.

Participating in sports is a fantastic way to keep your stress levels at bay. Plus while you are exercising you have time to think about your day and plan it out.

Another reason why you should start adding some type of sporting activity into your life is that it can become a family affair. One of the biggest problems for families today is that everyone is running around at warp speed.

Taking time out to do sports together is a great way to make sure you spend enough time with your family. The best way to ensure this happens regularly is to schedule your sporting time on your family calendar. Plus make it a priority.

Sports that you can do to help balance your life include swimming, walking, running, skating, cycling, dancing and even things like taking part in a family cross-fit class.

Adding sports into your life is beneficial for all family members. Even young children and especially teenagers can be dealing with a ton of stress. They may feel pressured into performing well at school and then add peer and social pressure on top of this. The rates of suicide amongst teenagers is at an all time high!

Sports can help everyone to relax and to just have fun. Whatever sport you choose it doesn't have to be a competitive one. Making it fun for every family member is important. You could even set up an obstacle course in your backyard and have timed runs. Younger children could have easier obstacles and don't forget to have some type of prize at the end! A free movie pass to see a movie of their choice is a great idea.

If you are feeling extremely stressed out then you may want to take up something like yoga. This is a fantastic way to help your body and your mind relax. There are many types of yoga available and not all involve deep meditation.

So why not think about adding some type of sporting activity into your life and make it an event your entire family can enjoy.

CHAPTER 7

GETTING THAT BALANCE
WORKING FOR YOU

To successfully balance your life and feel as though you are accomplishing your desires there are several things you can start to do. One of the first ones is to simply create a schedule.

If you haven't used a calendar then you should start using one. It is an easy way to see what you have going on and when. Plus it allows you to make time for those important things in life.

You should try and use two different calendars, one for work and one for your personal life. When you have a large project to complete start planning it out and allotting time on your calendar.

Schedule in your breaks and be aware of any appointments or errands that you have to run immediately after work. This way, when you know you have to pick up your children, you won't be tempted to stay a few minutes longer at work.

For your home calendar get into the habit of scheduling family time, along with time for housework, shopping and some alone time, just for you! When you do this you will know that your child has a baseball game that you don't want to miss. Simply schedule this time on your work calendar as well, so you don't forget!

Another way to get a balance between work and home is to avoid as many distractions and interruptions as possible. Maybe you can put your phone onto voice mail, or use headphones if the office is busy.

One huge distraction is your inbox. You don't have to check your mail every 10 minutes. Instead make a habit of only checking it just a few times per day. This way you won't be tempted to start answering unnecessary emails or start chatting with a friend.

This next item is super important and has to do with your mindset. Stop thinking that you have to be working on overdrive, or that you have to be a superman or woman. You don't and you can only accomplish so much each day.

Don't get into the habit of skipping your breaks or working through lunch. Instead always make a point of taking these breaks and recharge and refuel. You will find that your energy and concentration levels are renewed.

In addition to this learn to say 'no'. You don't have to accept every invitation you receive, and you don't have to always be the parent that volunteers at school. You will have more peace of mind when you refuse certain things and only take on those that you truly have time for.

CHAPTER 8

FINDING TIME IN YOUR BUSY SCHEDULE

Do you feel as though you are running around like crazy, you feel as though you are being pulled in all directions, and don't know where to turn next? This is not an uncommon feeling and is a sign that you need to discover ways to free up time in your busy schedule.

When you have achieved a work - life balance you will be enjoying life every day. You can handle pretty much anything that life throws at you, you are happy and content with the person that you are.

To find time in your schedule you need to try and find a way to remove unnecessary things. Your goal should be to live a much simpler life.

To achieve this try and make a list of all the things that are important to you. Then narrow this list down again and have just two or three main priorities in your life. Just doing this removes a ton of stress and gives you more time.

For example you may be trying to juggle work, studying for a degree after work and saving for a new home, as well as spending time with your family. If you are feeling overwhelmed with all of this is there something that you can put on the back burner for a while?

Is studying for your degree just an interest or a way to get that new home? If it is only for your pleasure can you spend less time on it or put it off for a year. This would free up your time to focus on saving for your home or having more family time.

Once you can limit some of your activities you will find that having more free time makes you feel happier and more relaxed. You automatically feel less stressed because you can envision getting home and playing with your children before they go to bed.

Sometimes it can definitely be difficult to cut things out of your schedule. If your work hours are getting longer and longer, take a look at what you do all day. Actually write out a calendar and allocate times to everything you do.

Say you work from 8am to 4pm - write down everything you do for a couple of days. This way you can see any patterns emerging. At the end of the day you can tally up how much time you spend on certain projects and how much time you spend on emails. You may be surprised at what you discover. Then see what you can cut back on so you can leave work at the right time each day.

CHAPTER 9

DOES YOUR LIFE FEEL
LIKE RUNNING A MARATHON?

When you are attempting to balance your life and your career you are often left feeling as though you are running a marathon. You just keep going and going and never seem to find, let alone reach, the finish line.

At work you may face a full calendar of meetings and deadlines for projects. While at home you have children to take to after school activities, homework to deal with and more. Let alone laundry, grocery shopping and dinner preparations.

When you feel so overbooked a natural reaction is to start putting more hours in to get everything done. You may find yourself staying later at work, or you may stay up late at night to finish that load of laundry.

Most people are struggling to find a way to balance their work and their personal life. Many actually have this as a priority over making more money or getting that promotion. They are looking for balance!

In order to stop running that marathon and never finishing it you need to take a good look at your life. Has your 40 hour work week manifested into a 60 hour week? The question you need to ask yourself is why? What has happened in order for you to spend that additional time at work.

One of the first things to look at is your time management skills. Are you spending too much time checking your email, do you sneak on social media sites? It is amazing how much time can be wasted by doing menial tasks.

Instead of arriving at work and checking your email, prioritize what you have to get done that day. What is the one biggest project that must be accomplished? Then simply get it done! Put off checking emails and other items until this project is finished. At least you now know you won't have to work late because of the fear of missing a deadline.

Each morning create a list of what has to be done and when. Always move the less important items to after lunch.

You can apply these same techniques to your home life. When you get home concentrate on getting the main things done first. This might be cooking dinner or taking your child to an appointment.

Leave the things that can wait until later on, try leaving them until the weekend. If you can do this then you know that job wasn't as important as you thought.

Just by making a few changes in how you look at things you can actually cross that finish line!

Printed by Libri Plureos GmbH in Hamburg,
Germany

9 789479 586451